D0604643

The Thousand Islands
Unforgettable

Photographs by George Fischer

Introduction & text by Anthony Mollica Jr.

NIMBUS PUBLISHING

CAPT. THOMSON'S WORLD RENOWNED
MOTOR BOAT TOURS
of THE 1000 ISLANDS

LEAVING FROM THE
CROSSMON HOUSE DOCK
ALEXANDRIA BAY, N. Y.

Daily 9:30 A. M. and 2:30 P. M. during June
During July and August 9:30, 10:30, 11:30, 1:30, 2:30, 3:30, 4:30
SUBJECT *to* CHANGE

LINE IS OPERATED BY
CAPTAIN C. S. THOMSON MOTOR BOAT TOURS, INC.

THE MOST DELIGHTFUL TRIP IN ALL THE WORLD

-- FARE $1.50 --

Tourists' Tickets issued by any booking agencies will be accepted

---

THE MOST DELIGHTFUL TRIP IN ALL THE WORLD

"That's how my grandfather, Capt. C. S. Thomson,
described his 1000 Islands boat tour in 1926."

— Capt. Ronald G. Thomson

Seems that things haven't changed in more than 80 years.

A 1000 Islands Tradition Since 1926

www.usboattours.com
1-800-253-9229

The Thousand Islands
Unforgettable

Photographs by George Fischer

Introduction & text by Anthony Mollica Jr.

The Great Lakes are the world's largest reservoir of freshwater. Together they drain more than four hundred thousand square miles of the North American continent. The lakes serve as a series of natural filtering bowls that steadily send crystal clear water eastward to the Atlantic Ocean. The final seven hundred fifty miles of this journey is through the St. Lawrence River.

One of nature's most spectacular celebrations is found within the first fifty miles of the St. Lawrence River where eighteen hundred islands are scattered in a remarkable maze of beauty. This very special portion of the river is known as the Thousand Islands, one of nature's great gifts to North America.

The River's outlet to the Atlantic Ocean beckoned early adventurers to enter and explore. Jacques Cartier was the first of several French explorers to journey against the current and travel five hundred miles into the great River. The River's swift rapids prevented his large ships from proceeding further. A few years later French explorer Samuel de Champlain traveled further reaching Lake Ontario and is remembered as the first European to observe the Thousand Islands.

The geological force that created the islands resulted from erosion produced by the melting ice sheets from the last great ice age 10,000 years ago. The volume of water cascading through this narrow valley produced deep channels leaving a multitude of granite peaks, today's islands.

By the mid-1800s wealthy sportsmen began to rediscover the Thousand Islands region as a paradise for boating and fishing. Much of the credit for the early surge in popularity belongs to George Pullman, the industrialist who developed the railroad sleeping car. In 1872 Pullman invited the United States President, Ulysses S. Grant, to his island to enjoy a few days of great fishing. The President, along with the normal contingent of Washington reporters, accepted Pullman's invitation. Every day the national news included reports of the region's natural beauty and the President's remarkable catches of fish. Millions of readers were learning about the Thousand Islands for the first time and decided to visit the region themselves.

The result was a tourist boom to the region. Many of North America's wealthiest businessmen including Nathan Strauss of Macy's, Charles Emery of American Tobacco, Frederick Bourne of Singer Sewing Machine, William Wyckoff of Remington Typewriter, George Boldt of the Waldorf-Astoria, Alexander R. Peacock of Carnegie Steel, Banker Charles Hayden and many others purchased islands to build summer homes.

The Thousand Islands boom of the late 1800s created a demand for resort hotels. Remarkable fishing adventures, fabulous steam yachts, magnificent summer homes and the

unforgettable natural beauty were part of each day's experience in the Thousand Islands. The new luxury hotels were considered to be among the finest resorts in North America.

The private island residences became symbols of the owner's creativity and wealth by having their architects create structures that were grand and unusual. The tradition of building unique summer homes in the Thousand Islands continues with the magnificent island structures of the past providing a backdrop for distinctive new homes. Each island becomes a singular natural location where owners are motivated to build enchanting summer homes in a variety of styles and sizes to the delight of all who cruise nearby. The summer homes range from the charming gingerbread cottages in Thousand Islands Park to impressive stone castles of monumental proportions. The Thousand Islands is one of the world's most picturesque and attractive waterways where beauty is everywhere and the water remains crystal clear and inviting.

The great St. Lawrence Seaway is navigated daily by huge ships from all parts of the world as well as luxury yachts, family cruisers, classic wooden runabouts and a wide range of rowing craft. The Thousand Islands is a boater's dream come true.

There are delightful communities all along the Canadian and American sides of the River with inviting harbor facilities. In addition there are an abundance of state and national parks with superb camping facilities. The abundance of comfortable tour boats provides visitors with an unforgettable experience that often includes visits to Boldt and Singer Castles. One of the memorable highlights of the region is to experience the exhibits at the Antique Boat Museum. Here visitors can learn about the history of the region and see the world's finest collection of vintage recreational watercraft including the thrill of a vintage speedboat ride.

George Fischer's magnificent photography captures the beauty and temperament of the Thousand Islands. The images of exhilarating summer, tranquil fall and spring provide a glimpse of why visitors to the Thousands Islands return again and again, year after year.

— *Anthony S. Mollica, Jr.*

Freighters from distant lands pass under the Thousand
Islands Bridge in the American Narrows.

With Boldt Castle looming in the background, classic boats and large ships travel through the Thousand Islands.

Boldt's Yacht House provided living quarters for his yacht crew.

The observation tower in the residence wing of the Boldt Yacht House offers a great view of the Castle and the Wellesley Island properties.

As the sun rises, the early morning mist begins to burn off the river near Brockville.

This summer cottage close to the Thousand Islands Bridge nearly covers the entire island.

Cherry Island's beautiful Casa Blanca, one of the most photographed homes on the River.

A colorful scene in the quaint village of Sackets Harbor.

Intricate fretwork trim is a common tradition among
Thousand Island homes and boathouses.

One of Cape Vincent's magnificent homes.

Watching from the upper level of this Westminster Park boathouse as the family sea skiff heads out for a cruise.

This large classic runabout heads downriver at high speed with a freighter in the distance.

Anna, the classic 1895 St. Lawrence rowing Skiff was built by Wilbur & Wheelock in Clayton and is still in regular use by its owner.

The Antique Boat Museum's classic 42' commuter, *Zipper*, glides past Rock Island Lighthouse.

The impressive stone Watergate on Heart Island was constructed as the intended formal entrance for boating guests to Boldt's chateau.

Summer visitors to the Thousand Islands believe that sunsets are more spectacular here than anywhere else.

The American span of the Thousand Island
Bridge connects Interstate Route 81 to
Wellesley Island and provides a marvelous
image during a mid summer sunset.

This span of the Thousand Islands Bridge becomes a spectacular illuminated arch over the American Narrows section of the Seaway at dusk.

Watching a great ship pass by from various ports around the world is a pleasant pastime for Thousand Islanders. This ship is traveling upriver in the beautiful American Narrows section of the Seaway between the mainland and Wellesley Island.

The great blue herons are a frequent sight in the Thousand Islands.

This group of seven beautiful islands is part of a section of River properties that are often referred to as "Millionaires Row".

Boldt Castle's charming reception room is fully restored and furnished along with the great hall and grand staircase.

This spectacular image shows the life size figures of three stags created to represent mythical heaven and light on top of the massive stone Watergate entrance to Heart Island and Boldt Castle.

Deer enjoy the good life living in large numbers on Wellesley Island.

Every fall, the trees on Heart Island become vibrant swatches of color preparing the Castle for winter on the River.

In spectacular fashion, a vintage Gar Wood runabout traveling at high speed slices through the waves from a passing tour boat.

An interesting glimpse of the magnificent classic boats
displayed in Clayton's popular Antique Boat Museum.

Carefully preserved wooden boats like this vintage Old Town canoe and this 1938 Chris-Craft
have become an important part of the traditional boating culture of the Thousand Islands.

A close up view of the forward section of the St. Lawrence rowing skiff showing its lapstrake construction of overlapping cedar planks.

An interesting view of Singer Castle from a classic wooden boat.

Singer Castle's rugged stone boathouse was built for Frederick Bourne,
the CEO of the Singer Sewing Machine Company.

Three classic wood boats. From the left, a 16' St. Lawrence Skiff, a 28' 1909 Numbers Boat, a 1932 25' Gar Wood runabout.

Swimming or playing in the crystal clear water of the St. Lawrence River is always a refreshing treat.

The cottage on Zavikon Island enjoys a great deal of attention all summer long from tour boat announcers who love to point out to passengers that the bridge connecting it to a tiny islet close by, is the shortest international bridge in the world. So they say.

Four miles west of Wolfe Island is tiny Pigeon Island with its unusual steel frame light tower. The stairway to the light and the watch room is enclosed within the large steel tube in the middle of the steel frame.

Estrellita (Little Star in Spanish) is a small island off of the foot of Fairyland Island with a large, magnificent summer home. Estrellita was built by Andrew Schuler, known in America as "The Potato Chip King," because he was the creator of Schuler's Potato Chips.

The full moon of a summer night shines brightly above the Boldt Castle spires.

The magnificent glass skylight in Boldt Castle illuminates the grand staircase and the central core of the building.

During the frigid North Country winter, the great River surrounds
Heart Island in ice while the lights remain bright.

Shadows form fascinating flowing patterns
on the midwinter snowfall near Kingston.

The city hall of Kingston is viewed
through a snow castle, built during
the winter carnival of Feb Fest.

Downtown Kingston's outdoor ice rink is ready for the city's annual Feb Fest celebration.

The intersection of King and Market Streets is a perfect setting for lively entertainment on a winter night.

Downtown Brockville, where the older buildings have been thoughtfully preserved.

Boldt's Clock Tower/Powerhouse was designed to appear like a small castle rising from the River depths and connected to Heart Island by a stone footbridge.

An interesting view of the marvelously steep and complex Boldt Castle roof with its multiple dormers, chimneys and spires.

Scenes in Brockville, Ontario where George Fulford created
his patent medicine that he sold worldwide.

These devilish gargoyles provide an interesting feature in
the delightful gardens at the *Fulford Place Museum*.

This popular Sackets Harbor restaurant provides the option of a beautiful outdoor garden to enjoy a meal within the lush summer foliage of the region.

The face of a grotesque gargoyle waterspout in a seashell adds a bit of drama to Boldt's garden fountain.

The Scenic Thousand Islands Parkway provides these cyclists a beautiful view of the St. Lawrence River and waterfront homes.

What could be better on hot summer's day than jumping in the crystal clear water of the St. Lawrence River.

Two inviting chairs on a dock are an invitation to sit for a while and relax watching the ships cruise by.

Islanders love to paint their traditional wood chairs in a variety
of bold colors encouraging friends to stop and visit.

The adjoining boathouses of Thousand Island Park use different colors to add a bit of frivolity as well as helping each boater identify their slip.

Summers in the Thousand Islands are filled with joy; Skiffing at Grenadier Island and the always delightful gingerbread cottages of Thousand Island Park.

The ornamental design of Sweetheart Cottage's upper porch, and the bicycles on the porch that are the islanders favorite form of transportation.

One of the three large sailing vessels at the pier is the famous schooner, *Pride of Baltimore*, effectively used as a training ship for young sailors.

This vintage boathouse on Cherry Island is part of the Casa Blanca estate. Like many of the older boathouses on the River it has complete living quarters on the upper floor for the estate owner's domestic staff or for extra guests.

This lovely vintage wood-canvas canoe is equipped with a special rowing seat and spoon-bill oars to provide the opportunity for pure exercise as well as for leisurely exploration.

From inside the old Cornwall Brothers Store Museum in Alexandria Bay, we can see the tour boat, *Alexandria Belle*, passing by with Boldt Castle in the distance.

The former Cornwall Brothers Store has become the Town of Alexandria Museum. This vintage St. Lawrence rowing skiff, fitted out with suitable fishing gear and the fishing guide's picnic basket, is one of several popular displays in the Museum.

The bow rises as this long vintage runabout gains speed on it's way to reach Boldt Castle ahead of the big tour boat.

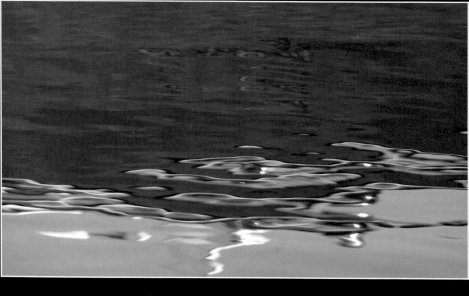

This handsome sailboat is cruising past Sisters Island Lighthouse built in 1870 just off the foot of Grenadier Island and just within the U.S. side of the international boundary.

The Prescott Harbor lighthouse is a 40-foot high replica of the original lighthouse built with funds donated by the local Rotary Club Members as a tourist information center.

The modern 730-foot Great Lakes ship, *Lake Michigan*, one of the largest cargo freighters serving the St. Lawrence Seaway system, always attracts attention.

In recent years visitors to the Thousand Islands have had the opportunity to enjoy sightings of Great Bald Eagles that nest along the St. Lawrence River.

The *Seth Green* is a modern 46-foot Research Trawler that is based in Cape Vincent by the New York State DEC to provide vital information necessary to maintain the quality of Lake Ontario's fish resources.

A family of Canada Geese also enjoy the abundance of natural resources common to the Thousand Islands region.

The Thousand Islands is filled with hundreds of ideal locations for Bass fishing. The tranquility in this early morning photograph is why the region enjoys being one of North America's most popular locations for tournament fishing.

The lighthouse at Tibbetts Point marks the entrance to the St. Lawrence River from Lake Ontario. It has become a popular location attracting more than 15,000 visitors each summer to enjoy fresh air and the wonderful view. During the summer season the lighthouse keeper's cottage is a hostel where youth from around the world have the opportunity to experience first hand being a light keeper for a night.

Two wonderful views of the Rock Island Lighthouse located just across the Seaway channel from the gingerbread community of Thousand Island Park. The lighthouse had to be built on a 30-foot man-made stone pier to make sure ships avoided the rocky shoals as they entered the American Narrows heading downriver.

Sunken Rock Lighthouse located almost directly across the Seaway from Boldt Castle guides huge freighters and pleasure craft safely past a dangerous shoal near Alexandria Bay.

The multitude of islands provides sailors with hundreds of lovely bays for pleasant overnight anchoring as well as a large number of state parks and national parks with excellent marina facilities.

A spectacular view of the Canadian shore and the two Canadian spans of the Bridge from the 1000 Islands Skydeck on Hill Island.

The sturdy little Hutchinson sport boat built in 1939 scoots past the huge Great Lakes freighter, *Saginaw*, heading for Duluth, Minnesota.

A dramatic mid summer sunset in
the Thousand Islands.

Sitting in the aft cockpit of a vintage mahogany runabout traveling at
high speed in the Thousand Islands is a thrill never to be forgotten.

The famous Clock Tower/Powerhouse is an important feature of the Boldt Castle compound on Heart Island.

The island emerges in the soft pastel colors of a misty morning in the Brockville Narrows.

A gathering of the fleet of seven Uncle Sam Tourboats by Harbor Island
and the Manhattan Island Group in the early morning.

Beautiful triple deck tourboats like the Island Princess provide marvelous experiences to the most popular locations in the Thousand Islands.

Three beautiful classic wooden boats, *Zipper, Gadfly* and *Teal* from the Antique Boat Museum's "in-water fleet", cruise past on their way to an island wedding.

A gathering of three classic boats at the boathouse of Acorn Lodge, Wellesley Island.

Watching the sunset in the Thousand Islands is a delightful way to end an active day on the River.

A view of the parlor in Oak Lodge on Wellesley Island. This wonderful home was built in 1902 with sixteen bedrooms.

Frederick Bourne's summer home on Dark Island was originally called the Towers. Today it's known as Singer Castle.

One of the older homes in Brockville that has become
a favorite Bed & Breakfast Inn for visitors.

The Fulford Place mansion, owned and operated by the Ontario Heritage Trust, has become a charming Museum in Brockville.

The Fulford Place Museum is the former home of George Taylor Fulford who made millions of dollars producing Pink Pills for Pale People in Brockville.

The Thousand Islands Winery thrives in the nearly ideal conditions of the Thousand Islands growing season.

This attractive footbridge connects Cherry Island with Isle Helena, a man-made islet that at one time held the owner's tennis court.

Once the Union Hotel in Sackets Harbor, this historic stone building (1817) is now the Seaway Trail Discovery Center & Gift Shop that is open all year.

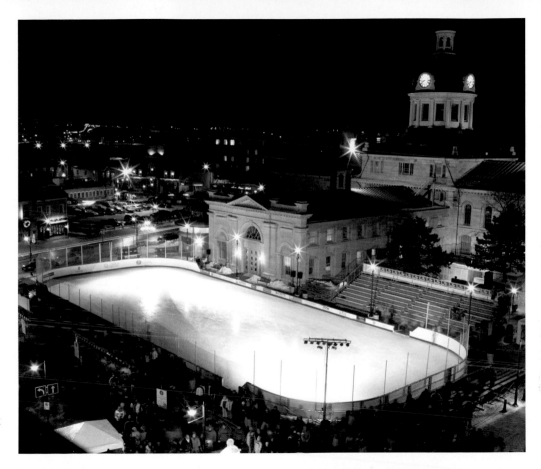

The outdoor
hockey
tournament in
downtown
Kingston is
another
traditional event
during Feb Fest.

Winter comes to Thousand Island Park on Wellesley Island and nearly all of the cottages are securely closed and carefully winterized until spring arrives.

On a bright, crisp winter's day, everyone loves
to ice skate in Kingston.

The weathered doorway
from an old motel cabin
near Alexandria Bay is a
reminder of times past.

The Asselstine Woolen Mill is
a popular exhibit building in
Upper Canada Village.

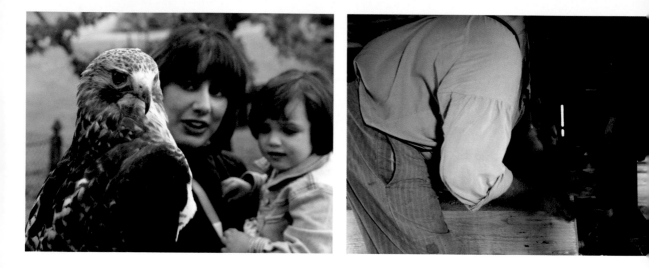

A visit to the Watertown Zoo is always
a delightful treat for the family.

A wagon load of fresh shorn wool on its way to the old
wooden woolen mill in Upper Canada Village.

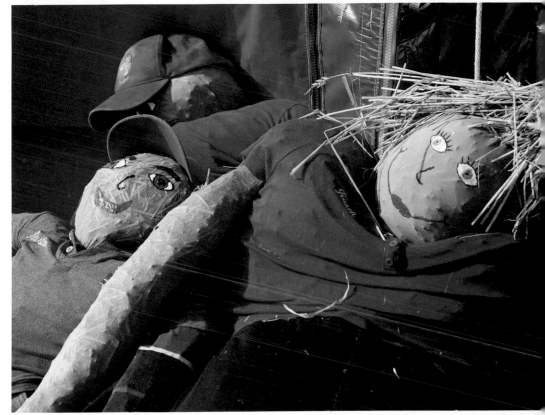

With three landmark spires, the main one being the tallest church spire in the Thousand Islands, the old First Presbyterian Church in Brockville is a major feature of this River community.

This restored home was the Commandant's headquarters during the War of 1812 in Sackets Harbor.

Interior of Senator George Fulford's magnificent home in Brockville. *Fulford Place*, was donated by his son to the Ontario Heritage Trust in 1987 and is now one of the region's most popular Museums.

In Alexandria Bay, the historic home of Captain Visger, one of the region's tour boat pioneers, has become a delightful bed & breakfast inn furnished in lovely period antiques.

The *Pride of Baltimore* under full sail cruises the St. Lawrence Seaway during its goodwill summer cruise through the Great Lakes.

A close up view of the *Pride of Baltimore* with two of her crew getting her ready for the next stop on her summer journey.

On the southwest point of Simcoe Island, which is about nine miles west of Kingston, is the light named for its location. Standing forty feet above the island's surface, Nine Mile Point Lighthouse was built in 1833 using rubble stone construction.

The constant current in the St. Lawrence River offers vacationers crystal clear water that is ideal for swimming.

The interesting seascape of the St. Lawrence River region often attracts a wide variety of unusual character vintage boats.

The state and national parks throughout the Thousand Islands provide excellent camp sites and most have support facilities which are carefully monitored all during the summer season.

The Thousand Islands offers recreational kayakers one of the finest venues in North America for this popular sport.

Alexandria Bay's Sunken Rock Lighthouse is located across the channel from Boldt Castle and has operated with solar power since 1988.

Heading downriver, the American Narrows section of the St. Lawrence Seaway begins with the 40-foot high Rock Island Lighthouse directly across the River from Thousand Island Park.

At sunset, from Nine Mile Point on Lake Ontario, we look across the length of the vast lake at a foreboding sky.

The River becomes very peaceful in the early morning stillness. This view, from a balcony at the Edgewood Resort, faces the old boathouses on Cherry Island with Cuba Island, Devil's Oven and Wellesley Island in the distance.

Looking upriver, between the Edgewood Resort and Cherry Island, where historic boathouses also provided living quarters for domestic staff to reside during the busy summer season.

From the upper deck of the tour boat, we see Boldt's Clock Tower which was built on a shoal, appearing to rise right from the water.

A small cruiser enjoys the tranquility of a secluded sand beach on Grenadier Island.

Vintage boats have remained very popular in the Thousand Islands and they are maintained in pristine condition so that they can be used regularly and often participate in classic boat shows.

Modern building materials have helped make kayaks less expensive and very popular. The Thousand Islands has become a favorite location for kayakers who enjoy the scenic islands, bays and channels where there is so much to see and enjoy.

This aerial view of Brockville shows the delightful geographic setting among the islands of this popular River community.

Windmill Point lighthouse is located just west of Cornwall, Ontario. It was originally built by a private owner as a windmill to crush wheat. The 80-foot stone tower was converted to a lighthouse by the Canadian government in 1874 to aid navigation on the upper section of the St. Lawrence River.

The historic stone flower mill of
S. J. Bellamy is an important exhibit
building in Upper Canada Village.

In Upper Canada Village there is much to see and opportunities to ride in vintage transportation.

The good news is that bald eagle sightings have become more frequent in the Thousand Islands in recent years. However, naturalists monitoring the eagles still feel that it is vital not to reveal their nesting locations to provide them with secluded sanctuaries.

Years ago island homes often needed a tower to provide pressure for running water. The more elaborate towers had lookouts to provide a view of the River as well. This classic old tower on Calumet Island has received very good care and is one of the few that remain today.

Nathan Strauss, the CEO of Macy's, built this 50-room home on Cherry Island in 1900. The cottage named Belora is still remarkably original and still furnished in the same manner as it has been since it was constructed.

As daybreak approaches, Heart Island and Boldt Castle begin to emerge with the dock lights glowing in the morning mist.

As evening approaches, a passenger in the classic 42-foot commuter cruiser, "Zipper", enjoys a spectacular view of the Thousand Islands sunset.

Alexandria Belle is one of the most popular tour boats in the Thousand Islands. It's an attractive replica of a Mississippi-style riverboat in the Uncle Sam Fleet operating out of Alexandria Bay.

The beautifully preserved old stone
mill at Upper Canada Village.

Her name is *Amaryllis* and she is a 106-foot houseboat. Built in Cape
Vincent in 1911, now permanently moored on Cobra Island.

198

The Thousand Islands region provides local and visiting artists with a multitude of inspirational subjects to expand their creativity and motivate their desire to produce.

This quiet River view is from inside the 106-foot houseboat *Amaryllis* that operates as a bed & breakfast inn.

Clayton's wonderful Handweaving Museum and Art Center has become a popular community institution.

A comfortable place in *Amaryllis* to sit and read or watch the shore birds.

Clayton's Handweaving Museum specializes in producing hand-woven fabrics and provides weavers with extensive resources to encourage the continuation of this traditional art form.

"Residents" of Upper Canada Village in period dress working at various activities common to this region a century ago.

Scenes from Upper Canada Village, just east of Morrisburg, where heritage homes were relocated during the construction of the Seaway and is now staffed by "residents" dressed in period costumes.

The Zina Hill Barbershop from the lost village of Moulinette has been accurately restored as it was in the late 1950s when the St. Lawrence Seaway Project displaced the entire village.

This plain white high gabled structure is the Sandtown Advent Church in the Lost Villages Museum. It was originally built around 1860 and is often used today for weddings and Advent Services.

The light generated by Ontario's Prescott Harbor Lighthouse with its powerful Fresnel lens can send a beam of light over 20 miles on a clear night.

The 40-foot Rock Island Lighthouse viewed from Wellesley Island helps guide ships traveling downriver safely into the Narrows toward Alexandria Bay.

The lighthouse at Nine Mile Point was built in 1833 and still serves as a guiding light for ships entering the St. Lawrence River from Lake Ontario near Kingston, Ontario.

One of the remaining cottages on Deer Island that belongs to the fascinating members of the mysterious Skull and Bones Society.

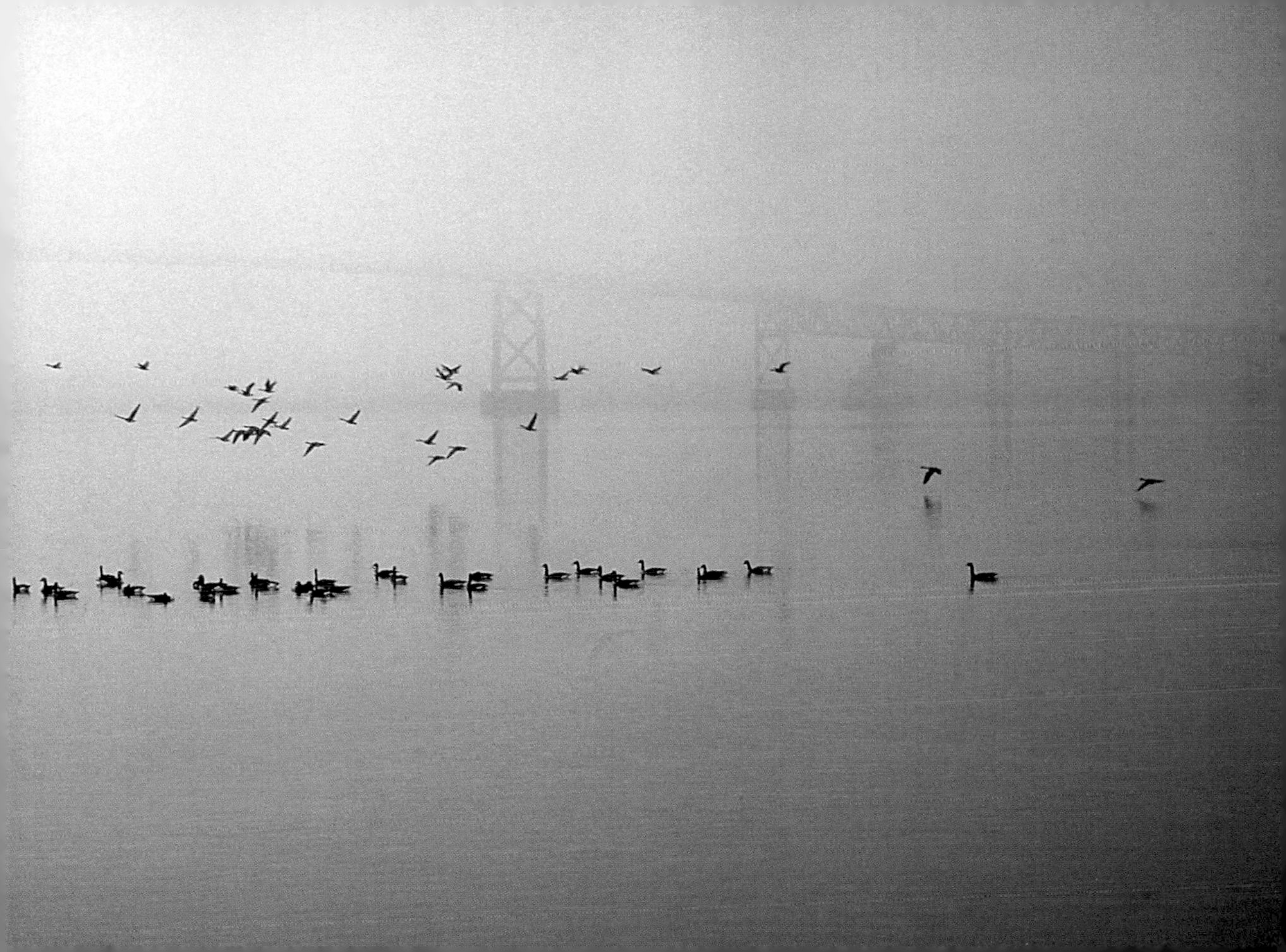

George Fischer is one of Canada's most celebrated and prolific landscape photographers. He has produced over thirty books and fifty fine art posters.

George's work has also appeared on the covers of numerous international magazines and newspapers, and in the promotional literature of tourism boards around the world. His most recent book, *Unforgettable Canada*, was on the *Globe and Mail's* bestseller list for eight weeks. George lives in Toronto.

See more of George Fischer's work at
www.georgefischerphotography.com

Anthony Mollica, Jr. has currently authored eight books devoted to significant American boat builders and the development of the Thousand Islands. He is an active trustee of the Antique Boat Museum in Clayton, NY and a popular speaker at marine museums and classic boat associations throughout North America. Since 1976 he and his family spend their summers at their cottage on Cherry Island near Alexandria Bay.

copyright © 2008 George Fischer
introduction and text © 2008 Anthony Mollica Jr.

Nimbus Publishing Limited
PO Box 9166
Halifax, NS B3K 5MB
902-455-4286

Printed in China

Design: Catharine Barker, National Graphics, Toronto, ON

Library and Archives Canada Cataloguing in Publication

Fischer, George, 1954-
The 1000 Islands : unforgettable / photography by George Fischer.

ISBN 978-1-55109-722-0

1. Thousand Islands (N.Y. and Ont.)--Pictorial works. I. Title.
II. Title: Thousand Islands.

FC3095.T43F583 2009   971.3'7050222   C2008-907519-6